DISCOVERING WORDS

NEEPIN AUGER

T0159914

RMB

apple **pomme** *picikwâs*

book

livre

masinahikan

canoe **canoë** *cîmân*

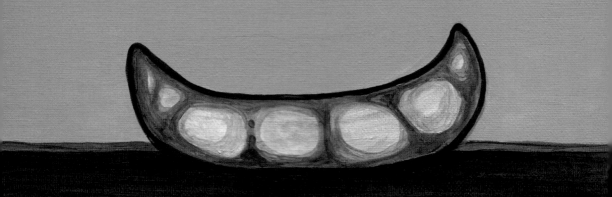

drum **tambour**

mistikwaskihkw

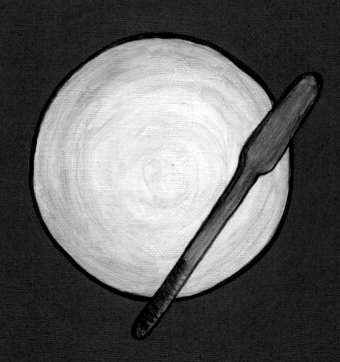

eggs **oeufs** *wâwa*

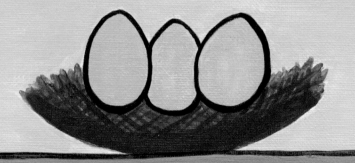

flower **fleur** *wâpikwaniy*

garden **jardin**

kiscikânis

hat **chapeau** *astotin*

igloo

igloo

miskwamiy ahpô koni wâskahikan

jacket **veste**

miskotâkay

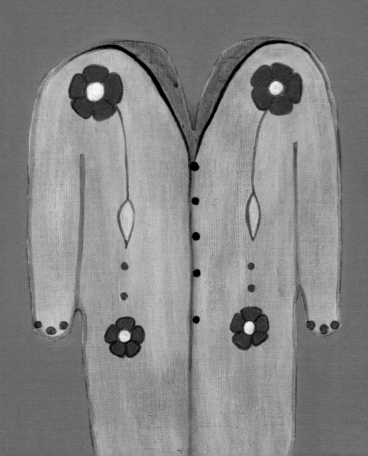

knife **couteau**

môhkomân

light **lumière** *wâskotêw*

moccasin **mocassin**

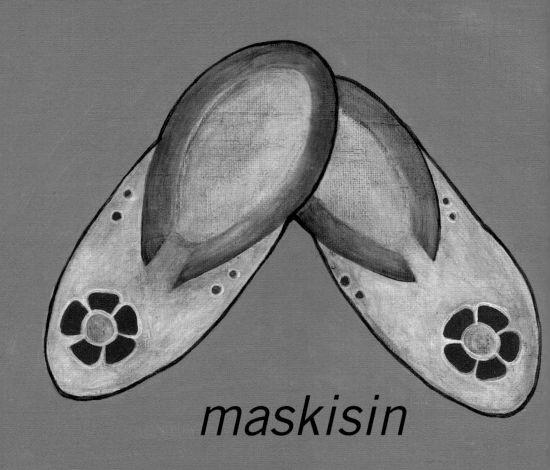

maskisin

night **nuit** *tipiskâw*

orange **orange** *osâwâs*

paintbrush **pinceau**

sisopêkahikanâhtikw

quilt **courtepointe**

nanâtohkokwâtêw

rainbow **arc en ciel**

pîsimoyâpiy

sweat lodge **suerie**

matotisân

teepee **tipi** *mîkiwâhp*

up to **jusqu' à** *ispimihk*

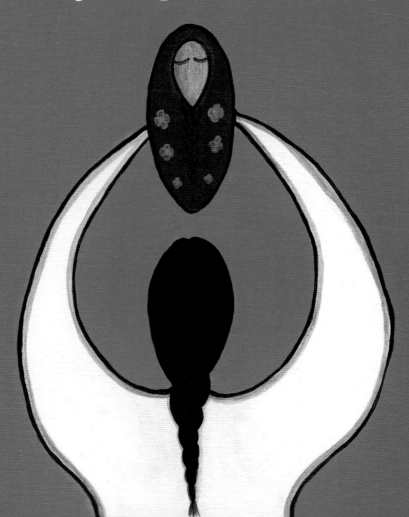

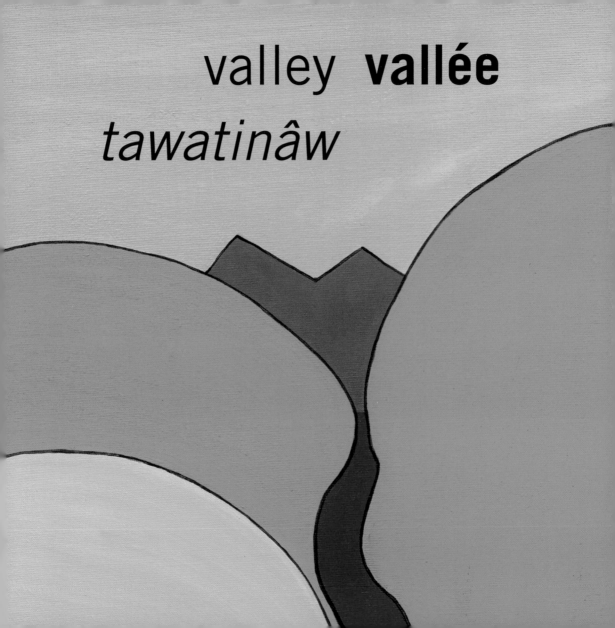

valley **vallée**

tawatinâw

water **eau** *nipiy*

x-ray **radiographie**

sâpwâpahcikan

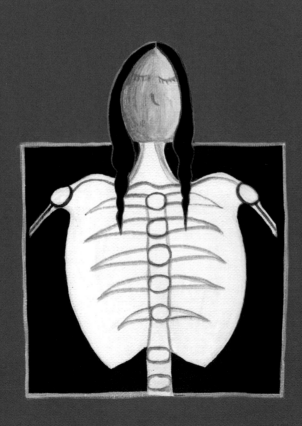

yoga

yoga

sêsâwîw

zig zag **zig zag**

wâwâkastêw

Pronunciation Guide

	apple	pomme pom	picikwâs pitsikwaas
	book	livre lee-vr	masinahikan musinuhikun
	canoe	canoë ka-no-ay	cîmân tseemaan
	drum	tambour tahm-boor	mistikwaskihkw mistikwuskeehk
	eggs	oeufs euh-f	wâwa waawu

flower	fleur	wâpikwaniy	
	fler	waapikwuneey	
garden	jardin	kiscikânis	
	zhar-dâh	kistsikaanis	
hat	chapeau	astotin	
	sha-po	ustotin	
igloo	igloo	miskwamiy ahpô koni wâskahikan	
	ee-gloo	miskwumeey uhpoo koni waaskuhikun	
jacket	veste	miskotâkay	
	vest	miskotaakay	
knife	couteau	môhkomân	
	koo-toe	moohkomaan	
light	lumière	wâskotêw	
	loo-mee-air	waaskotayoo	

	moccasin	mocassin	maskisin
		moh-ka-sah	muskisin
	night	nuit	tipiskâw
		nwee	tipiskaaw
	orange	orange	osâwâs
		oh-ron-zh	osaawaas
	paintbrush	pinceau	sisopêkahikanâhtikw
		pahn-so	sisopaykuhikunaahtik
	quilt	courtepointe	nanâtohkokwâtêw
		koor-teuh-pwant	nunaatohkokwaatayoo
	rainbow	arc en ciel	pîsimoyâpiy
		ark-ons-yel	peesimoyaapeey
	sweat lodge	suerie	matotisân
		soo-er-ee	mutotisaan

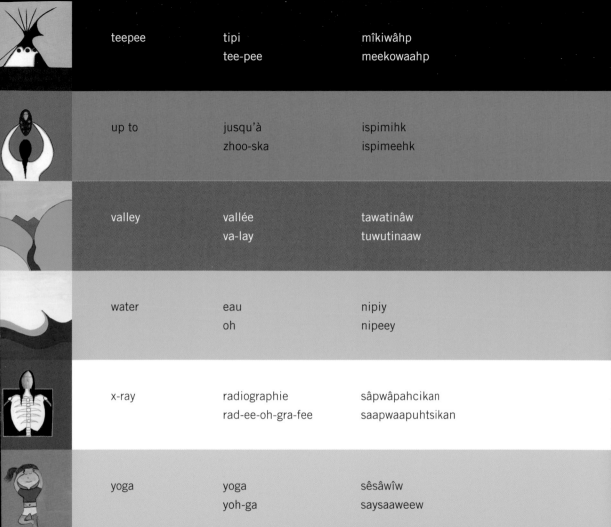

	teepee	tipi tee-pee	mîkiwâhp meekowaahp
	up to	jusqu'à zhoo-ska	ispimihk ispimeehk
	valley	vallée va-lay	tawatinâw tuwutinaaw
	water	eau oh	nipiy nipeey
	x-ray	radiographie rad-ee-oh-gra-fee	sâpwâpahcikan saapwaapuhtsikan
	yoga	yoga yoh-ga	sêsâwîw saysaaweew
	zig zag	zig zag zig-zag	wâwâkastêw waawaakustayoo

For my daughter Gracie

For information on purchasing bulk quantities of this book, or to obtain media excerpts or invite the author to speak at an event, please visit rmbooks.com and select the "Contact" tab.

RMB | Rocky Mountain Books Ltd.
rmbooks.com
@rmbooks
facebook.com/rmbooks

Cataloguing data available from Library and Archives Canada
ISBN 9781771604765 (paperback)
ISBN 9781771603294 (board book)
ISBN 9781771603300 (electronic)

Cree translations and pronunciations by Naomi McIlwraith and Cree Elder Elizabeth Letendre
French translations and pronunciations by David Warriner
Book design by Chyla Cardinal

Printed and bound in China

We would like to also take this opportunity to acknowledge the traditional territories upon which we live and work. In Calgary, Alberta, we acknowledge the Niitsitapi (Blackfoot) and the people of the Treaty 7 region in Southern Alberta, which includes the Siksika, the Piikuni, the Kainai, the Tsuut'ina and the Stoney Nakoda First Nations, including Chiniki, Bearpaw, and Wesley First Nations. The City of Calgary is also home to Métis Nation of Alberta, Region III. In Victoria, British Columbia, we acknowledge the traditional territories of the Lkwungen (Esquimalt, and Songhees), Malahat, Pacheedaht, Scia'new, T'Sou-ke and WSÁNEĆ (Pauquachin, Tsartlip, Tsawout, Tseycum) peoples.

We acknowledge the financial support of the Government of Canada through the Canada Book Fund and the Canada Council for the Arts, and of the province of British Columbia through the British Columbia Arts Council and the Book Publishing Tax Credit.

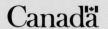